Sailing

Suzie
Porter

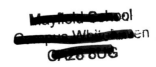

WAYLAND

Published in 2014 by Wayland

Copyright © Wayland 2014

Wayland   Wayland Australia
338 Euston Road   Level 17/207 Kent Street
London NW1 3BH   Sydney NSW 2000

Senior editor: Debbie Foy
Designer: Rebecca Painter
Photographer: Michael Wicks
Photoshoot co-ordinator: Jon Richards

Acknowledgements:
The author and publisher would like to thank the following people
for participating in our photoshoot: Lucy Scott, Eve Townsend and
Ben Townsend.

A special thank you to Emsworth Sailing Club for their help and advice.

All photography by Michael Wicks except
4 Dreamstime.com/Dwight Smith; 7 top Wang Song/Xinhua Press/Corbis
26 Dreamstime.com/Ahmad Faizal Yahya; 28 Getty/Alison Langley;
29 Dreamstime.com/Gabigarcia

British Library Cataloguing in Publication Data
Porter, Suzie.
Sailing. -- (Get outdoors)
1. Sailing--Juvenile literature.
I. Title II. Series
797.1'24-dc22

ISBN: 978 0 7502 8876 7

First printed in 2010 by Wayland

Printed in China

Wayland is a division of Hachette Children's Books,
an Hachette UK company.
www.hachette.co.uk

Contents

What is sailing? 4

Why go sailing? 6

How to get started 8

Sailing equipment 10

Understanding the wind 12

Getting afloat 14

Changing direction 16

Making a turn 18

In deep water! 20

The next step 22

On the open water 24

Competition racing 26

Sailing challenges! 28

Glossary 30

Further information 31

Index 32

What is sailing?

Sailing is a sport for everyone – no matter what their age or ability. A day on the water can mean anything from a family trip down the river to serious racing on the ocean. Once you know the basics there are endless possibilities for sailing fun!

The basics of sailing

Using a sail to catch the wind, a boat is propelled through the water as fast as the wind can carry it. As the wind affects how fast you go, you can use the sail to speed up, slow down and change direction. The **rudder** is also used to control the direction that the boat sails in, and works rather like a steering wheel does in a car.

Freedom on the water! Sailing boats come in many different shapes and sizes, with up to three sails.

Sailing in the past

A traditional sailing **dinghy** was originally made from wood with a simple cotton sail. They were used for transport across rivers and fishing in shallow waters. Although wooden boats are still used today for cruising trips and family days out, they are heavy and not as fast or strong as today's lighter weight boats that many people now enjoy racing. The fastest boats are the lightest, so most dinghies are now made from strong, light plastics.

In the past, sailing boats were made from wood and had cotton sails.

Types of sailing boats

Yachts are the largest types of boats, and can be used to sleep on or even live on. Dinghies are smaller and easier to manage, so most sailors learn how to sail in them. A dinghy can be **launched** and **recovered** from the water each time you use it, and is kept on a **trailer** on the land so is easy to move around and store. Dinghies typically only have one or two sails and space for one or two sailors, making them perfect for learning to sail with a friend or on your own. Boats with just one sail and space for one sailor are known as single-handed, while boats with an extra sail and space for two sailors are known as double-handed.

*In a single-handed (one-person) dinghy, the sailor controls the sail and steers the boat, so they are called the **helm**. The second sailor onboard a double-handed (two-person) boat controls the second extra sail, and is called the **crew**.*

Why go sailing?

If you're looking for a new sporting challenge and enjoy being around water, look no further than sailing! Although being afloat might take a little getting used to, before the end of your first day on the water you will be confident enough to go sailing on your own.

Physical and mental skills

Setting off on your first sailing adventure is an exhilarating and rewarding experience as you have to work on balance, control, concentration and other skills to speed through the water.

Sailing requires determination, skilled boat handling and confidence. Once you are happy with the basics, you will find yourself eager to try out other adventures on the water. Sailing is a challenging activity and you will never be bored. In fact, after just one session you will probably be hooked!

Just for fun

Sailing is the ideal way to get outdoors and be active without having to plan ahead too much. Sailing takes place anywhere that there is enough water to float a boat, including lakes, rivers, streams and oceans, so you can be sure that there will be a sailing club, school or training centre just down the road from you.

After a couple of lessons, you will be able to go on cruising adventures with your friends and family to discover new beaches and locations that you have never seen before.

Sailing is the perfect way to enjoy the outdoors with a group of friends at a local sailing club.

Going for gold

While many sail just for fun, some sailors enjoy adding a competitive edge to the sport. Dinghy racing takes place all over the country, and at every level, from local sailing club competitions to big international events.

The Olympic Games gathers together the very best sailors in the world to race against each other. Competitive sailing is not just about skills on the water, but also fitness, strength, stamina and racing tactics.

With three gold medal successes, Ben Ainslie is the most successful Olympic sailor of all time.

Warming up

Before you go sailing it is important to warm up your arms and legs, as you will be working these muscles hard. Pulling in the sails and leaning out of the boat to keep it as balanced as possible will put a lot of strain on your arms, stomach and thigh muscles.

Good warm-ups to run through include a gentle jog, making big circles with your arms to get the blood pumping, and squats and star jumps to get your legs ready to work.

How to get started

Anyone who enjoys being active and taking on a new challenge will enjoy the exhilaration that comes with single-handed or double-handed sailing. Start your sailing career in a responsible way by learning the techniques and safety advice from professionals. Ideally, you should also be able to swim at least 50 m (165 ft).

First time afloat

The best time to learn sailing is during the summer months when the weather and the water are relatively warm. Unlike indoors sports, sailing is reliant on the weather. You need wind to move the boat and clear skies to keep you warm. Although getting wet when sailing is inevitable, rainy conditions will make you cold and reduce visibility on the water, running the risk of accidents.

Always learn from a qualified instructor at a local sailing club. This way you will learn correct techniques and safety advice.

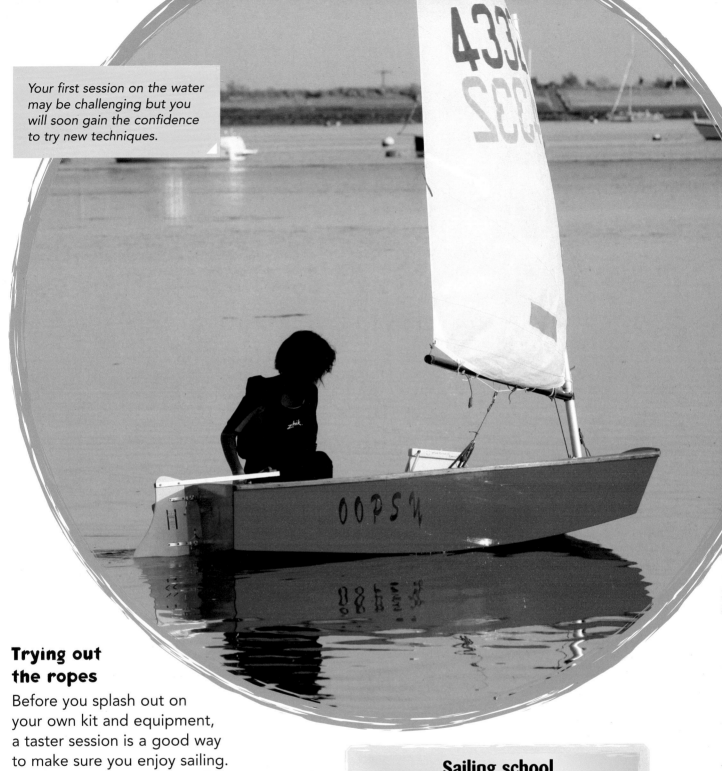

Your first session on the water may be challenging but you will soon gain the confidence to try new techniques.

Trying out the ropes

Before you splash out on your own kit and equipment, a taster session is a good way to make sure you enjoy sailing. Clubs and sailing centres offer short courses, often with a choice of sailing single-handed or in a bigger boat with an instructor. Most courses offer a combination of on-water training and classroom sessions to enable you to understand the technical side of sailing, too.

Sailing school

Sailing centres affiliated to the RYA (Royal Yachting Association) are found along the coast and at a number of inland lakes and reservoirs. These schools offer a safe introduction to sailing with lessons on land and on water. After a one-day session you may be happy sailing the boat on your own!

Sailing equipment

You will need a boat and some specialised gear, but at first you should be able to borrow everything from your sailing centre or school. There are technical names for each part of the boat, and it is important to know what these are when you are on the water.

Mainsail *The largest sail on the boat, attached to the boom and mast.*

Mast *The vertical pole that holds up the sail.*

Mainsheet *The rope used to pull in the mainsail.*

Jib *The smaller sail at the front of the boat. These only feature on double-handed boats.*

Boom *The horizontal pole that is attached to the bottom of the mainsail.*

Painter *The rope used to secure the boat to the land.*

Bow *The front of the boat.*

Hull *The main body of the boat.*

Dagger board *This helps to steer and balance the boat by moving up and down into and out of the water.*

What to wear

Sailing gear ensures you stay safe and comfortable on the water. As you become more interested in sailing, you may want to replace items borrowed from the sailing centre by buying your own.

Buoyancy aid *The most important piece of kit for sailing. Made from spongy foam, it will help you to float straight back up to the surface if you fall in or capsize.*

Gloves *These keep your hands warm and protect them from blisters when you are pulling ropes around the boat. They are normally made from a stretchy material with strong, protective fabric across the palms.*

Wetsuit *This tight-fitting suit goes on straight over your swimming costume, and is designed to let you get soaking wet without getting cold. The material allows water to seep in, holding it next to your skin to warm it up, and preventing more cold water from rushing in.*

Boots *These are made from the same material as the wetsuit. It is important to wear proper sailing boots as they allow your feet to get wet without getting cold, and protect your toes and the soles of your feet from getting injured on the boat.*

Tiller *This steers the boat.*

Rudder *This is attached to the tiller and controls the direction of the boat.*

Stern *The back of the boat.*

Safety first

If you fall overboard you do not have time to react as quickly as your buoyancy aid will, even if you are a strong swimmer. But your buoyancy aid needs to be a snug fit. If it's too big, it will float up over your head and not be effective. To check it's a good fit, make sure it will support your body weight. If you can pull it over your head, you need to tighten up the fastenings or wear a smaller size.

Understanding the wind

Getting to grips with wind direction is vital when learning to sail. When you are sailing you need to angle the sails in different ways depending on the wind and the direction you want to travel in.

Moving with the wind

When the wind hits the sail, it has the effect of pushing it over, as it would any other object. But thanks to the balance offered by the dagger board and rudder, it is kept slightly more balanced. By leaning your weight out over the side of the boat, you can balance out this pushing effect. By doing this you keep the boat upright, and let the power of the wind propel the boat forward.

wind direction

Wind direction

Look at a flag to find out the direction that the wind is blowing in. You cannot sail directly into the wind, so this angle (the angle that the flag is pointing in) will be one you need to avoid on the water. This is the **no-go zone**.

Close-hauled

Close-hauled is the closest you can get to sailing directly into the wind. If you want to sail to a point in the direction the wind is blowing in, you will be able to tightly zigzag your way almost directly towards it. To keep the boat balanced properly you will also need to have your **dagger board** down as far as possible while you sit up on the side of the boat.

For close-hauled sailing, your mainsail should be pulled in as far as possible to catch as much wind as you can.

wind direction

sailing direction

Beam reach

A **beam reach** is when the wind is blowing straight onto the side of the sail. If you want to sail in a forward direction you should be able to do this without having to shift direction or zigzag towards it. This is the easiest and fastest way of sailing. You should usually be sitting out on the side of the boat, but you won't have to work as hard as you do when sailing close-hauled.

Training run

A **training run** is where you are literally 'running away from the wind'. As well as letting the sails right out, you will also need to raise the dagger board almost completely up.

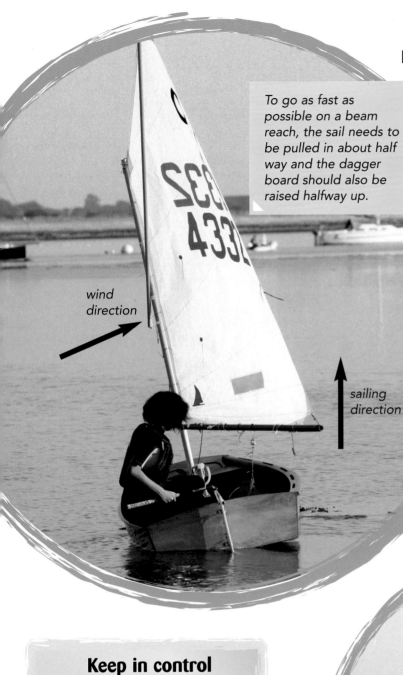

To go as fast as possible on a beam reach, the sail needs to be pulled in about half way and the dagger board should also be raised halfway up.

wind direction

sailing direction

On a training run, the wind blows over the back of the boat. You need to have the sail as far out as possible to catch the wind and be dragged forward.

Keep in control

When you sail too close to the wind, your sails will lose power and start flapping, slowing you down and maybe even causing you to stop moving completely. Sailing schools will often use the phrase: 'A flappy sail is an unhappy sail. Pull it in and make it grin!' to help remind you to keep your sail pulled in and as filled as possible.

wind direction

sailing direction

Each time you want to go sailing, your boat needs to be rigged. Rigging is putting together all sails and kit that are stored separately while the boat is ashore.

Rigging

All boats are different when it comes to **rigging**, but there are a few things you should always check. Before putting up the sail, make sure the boat is 'head to wind', which means that the front of the boat is pointing in the direction the wind is coming from.

While ashore you should hoist the mainsail and attach the rudder and tiller, to prepare as far as possible before the boat enters the water. Make sure that the mainsheet has a knot at the end, which will stop it from whipping out of your reach while sailing.

With the sail up, the rudder attached and the dagger board in place, this boat is ready to sail.

Safety checks

To avoid any accidents on the water, check that all the rigging ropes are stored tidily. Getting a foot or arm tangled in ropes is a danger – so stay alert!

Launching

Once your boat is rigged then you are ready to launch the boat into the water. Keep the boat head to wind to make sure that it does not sail away while you are still on land. Roll the trolley down the beach or slipway until the boat floats up on the water. Secure the boat by tying it to the side of the slipway or ask a friend to hold the painter while you return the trolley to a safe spot on the land. When you are ready to set off, simply untie the painter and push yourself away from the shore.

Aim to keep the boat facing into the wind as you walk towards the water.

Lower the trolley onto the water until the boat floats.

Getting afloat

As you leave the shore, sit on the side of the hull and face forwards. Keep an eye out for any other boats in the area. Remember to tuck your feet under the **toe straps**, as this will prevent you from falling backwards out of the boat.

Hold the mainsheet with your 'front' hand and the tiller with your 'back' hand.

Get a friend to hold the painter while you return the trolley to a safe place onshore.

As the helm of a single-handed boat you will be in charge of the mainsail, dagger board and tiller. The most efficient way to position yourself in the boat is to hold the tiller and steer with your hand nearest to the back of the boat. This means your 'front' hand is able to control the mainsail and dagger board, and allows you to sit facing forward in a comfortable way.

Changing direction

Sailing in a straight line is easy, but learning to change direction while sailing is more of a challenge. As you alter the angle of the boat towards the wind, your sail will automatically move with it, so you need to make sure you know how to adjust the positioning of the sail to keep your speed up.

Using the sail and tiller, you can turn your boat in any direction.

If you are sailing in one direction and want to turn round and sail the opposite way, you have two options for changing direction – **tacking** and **gybing**.

Tacking means turning a boat across the wind, with the wind blowing towards the front of the boat at all times. Gybing is when you change direction with the wind blowing onto the back of the boat.

To tack or to gybe?

If you are sailing close-hauled (roughly in the direction of the wind), you will need to remain as close-hauled as you can. To do this you will need to tack, as you want to keep pointing towards the wind. Tacking will move the boom from one side of the boat to the other, allowing the mainsail to fill up with wind again on the other side of the boat. This allows you to sail in a zigzag pattern.

*Changing direction, such as moving around a **mark**, requires you to pull in the sail and steer around with the tiller.*

Once the sail has swapped sides you need to move across the boat and rearrange your ropes ready to sail away.

The main differences

Tacking is the slowest and most steady way to change direction, as the bow of the boat moves through the wind, de-powering the sail and staying controllable. As gybing moves the stern of the boat through the wind, there is always wind in the sails, making it much quicker than tacking.

To change direction when you are downwind (when the wind is behind you), you have two options. One is to pull the sail in tight, which will automatically pull your boat in one direction. The other is to gybe, where the stern will move across the wind and the boom will cross to the other side of the boat, letting you sail in the opposite direction.

Making a turn

Tacking and gybing require slightly different movements but otherwise are quite similar. By following a simple step-by-step process you will be able to see just how easy it is.

First check the surrounding area for other boats. Then prepare to move into the centre of the boat.

Preparation

Hold the tiller in your 'back' hand and the mainsheet in your 'front' hand as this will help you stay in control. Ensure that the mainsheet is running freely and is not going to get caught as the sail moves across the boat. Look around to ensure you are clear to make the move.

Step-by-step tacking

1 Bring your body weight closer into the boat. If you have been sitting right on the edge, move further into the centre and slowly let the sail out.

2 Push the tiller as far away from you as possible and the boat will start to move into the wind. As the sail heads into the wind, it will move into the centre of the boat and lose power. Duck under the boom and cross to the other side of the boat.

3 Once on the other side of the boat, straighten up the tiller to head in the right direction and pull the sail back in.

Wait for the sail to move across and be prepared to duck under the boom.

Swap your hands so that your 'back' hand is holding the tiller again, and your 'front' hand is holding the mainsheet.

Once on the other side of the boat 'swap' hands so that your 'back' hand is holding the tiller.

① ② photos

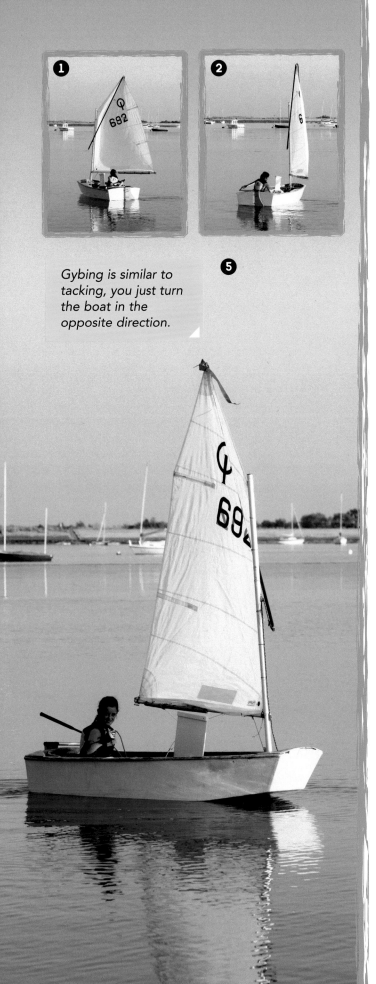

Gybing is similar to tacking, you just turn the boat in the opposite direction.

⑤

③ **④**

Step-by-step gybing

1 Move into the centre of the boat and bring the tiller close to you.

2 The boom will begin to move slowly into the centre of the boat.

3 Duck under the boom – it will move across the boat very quickly, as the wind moves to the other side of the sail.

4 Once the wind crosses the centre of the boat, move to the other side of the boat and straighten up your steering to point in the right direction.

5 Swap your hands so that your 'back' hand is controlling the tiller and your 'front' hand is holding the mainsheet.

Communication is the key!

Gybing and tacking involve a lot of movement around the boat, so everyone needs to know what is going to happen. If sailing single-handed, make sure you are prepared before making a turn. If sailing double-handed, be sure to let your crew know when you are making a turn so they can prepare the ropes. The helm needs to shout when they start the turn, so the crew can make sure they avoid the boom and move across the boat at the right time.

in deep water!

Sailing boats keep their balance by the body weight of the sailors and the force of the wind in the sails. If your boat isn't balanced you may capsize and it's essential to know what to do in this case. It's best to practise this drill before you actually have to use it!

Avoiding a capsize

The best way to avoid capsizing is to act quickly when the boat begins to lean towards the water, or heel over. To prevent a full capsize there are two things you should do. Firstly, lean as far out of the boat as possible, using the toe straps to keep you secure. You can also let out the sail slightly to spill some of the wind and regain your control.

If your boat capsizes and you cannot correct it, you should stay with the boat rather than try to swim to shore. You are more likely to be spotted by someone who can help.

Step-by-step capsize recovery

If you do capsize, don't panic. Here are the steps to take to right yourself when your sail hits the water:

Make sure that you are free of all ropes and fittings. Swim to the inside of the boat and push the dagger board all the way down.

Swim around to the under side of the boat and put your weight on the dagger board. In strong winds or with heavy boats you might need to climb up and stand on it to get enough weight to pull it up.

Use your weight to pull the boat upright.

As the boat rights itself, pull yourself into the hull.

Once back on board untangle ropes, check that the rudder and tiller are still in place and bail out any water in the bottom of the boat.

Turning turtle

Although many boats have floats to prevent them capsizing in strong winds and currents, there is a danger that a capsized boat will completely turn over, leaving the mast pointing directly downwards into the water. This is known as 'turning turtle', and is a little harder to correct than a simple capsize, although you should react in the same way. In this case, get hold of the mainsheet and use it to help pull the sail to the surface while you lean on the dagger board as hard as possible.

The next step

Once you are happy with the basics of sailing there are many more elements to try out to keep you on your toes, from double-handed sailing to trapezing, and even adding more sails to the challenge.

Trapezing allows you to use all your body weight to balance the boat.

Trapezing

Leaning out of the boat as far as possible lets you keep the sail pulled further in and catch as much wind as you can, making you sail faster. **Trapezing** enables you to lean out even further, letting you go even faster without losing control of the boat.

A trapeze is a harness that is attached to the boat by wires and enables the crew members to lean out of the boat to balance it. The trapeze itself is a stretch of elastic that runs from the top of the mast to the hull of the boat. Once you have hooked onto the trapeze you can stand on the side of the boat and lean out as far as you can, using the mainsheet to help you stay stable.

The trapeze harness has straps over the shoulders and around the waist, joining with a hook in the middle.

A trapeze harness is worn underneath your buoyancy aid.

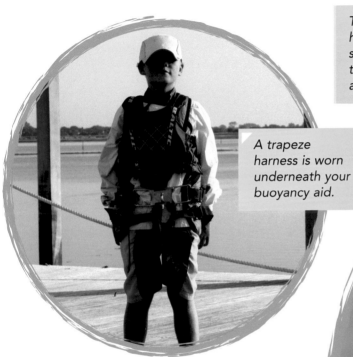

Spinnakers

Certain types of boats also have an extra sail called a **spinnaker**. This is used when you are sailing downwind, as it is designed to balloon with the wind and pull you along, but cannot be pulled in tight like the mainsail.

You pull on the spinnaker halyard (a rope that runs up the mast) to hoist the sail, and then use a pole to keep it sticking as far out of the boat as possible. By tweaking the spinnaker **sheets** you are then able to make sure the sail gets as full as possible. Once you are ready to change direction again, simply release the spinnaker halyard and drop the sail back into the pocket that it is stored in when not in use.

The spinnaker is an extra sail that is held out with a pole at the front of the boat.

On the open water

Once you have learnt the basics of sailing through a RYA sailing centre, you may have the desire to get out onto the open water. Proper planning for this kind of trip is essential, as is making sure you have all the necessary equipment in case of a sudden change in weather.

Day cruising

Although a lot of sailors enjoy the thrill of high-powered racing, if you are not interested in going as fast as possible then dinghy cruising is a great alternative. Rather than rushing around on the water, cruising is a great way to spend a leisurely day exploring the outdoors. You could pack up a picnic and go on a family adventure to a beach that cannot be reached by car, or you could go for a short sail to a local sandy beach for ice cream. The possibilities are endless.

What to take

Although you need to be prepared for every trip you take on the water, these new and exciting adventures require a bit more planning and some extra supplies. You need to make sure that you have all the equipment onboard that you might need in an emergency.

Extra food and water Sailing is very physical so you need to make sure that you keep your energy levels up by having some healthy snacks onboard and plenty of water in case it gets hot.

Emergency money and mobile phone It is important to have money with you in case you need extra supplies, and with a mobile phone you can keep in contact with people onshore at all times.

Sun protection The sun is even stronger when you are on the water so it is important to keep on reapplying sun block, even when the sun is not shining.

Personal medication In case you end up on the water for longer than you originally planned, it's best to take any personal medication with you, along with a first aid kit.

Spare jumper The wind can be very cold on the open water, so an extra jumper or fleece jacket will keep you warm.

Sun hat Protect your eyes and face from the sun and wind with a peaked cap.

Woolly hat Heat leaves your body quickest through your head, so on cold days pack a woolly hat.

Towel A spare towel is always a good idea for splashes or even capsizes.

Competition racing

Once you are skilled and confident on the water why not try out dinghy racing? Sailing is a competitive sport at many levels, from races at your local sailing club to Olympic and Paralympic events.

How racing works

For racing you need to be in complete control of your boat and understand the rules, so it's a good idea to take an initial course of lessons on racing with a qualified instructor. This will get you used to how dinghy racing works, explain the rules that will help you avoid a collision, and give you tips on going as fast as possible around the course.

*Racing events such as this **regatta** can be very busy, so it is vital you know all the rules of the event.*

Junior racing

The best way to get involved in junior racing is at your local sailing club. This will usually be open for children under the age of 18, and will often include race training sessions and classes to help you improve your skills as you gain confidence.

Rules and regulations

There are plenty of racing rules, but you only need a few to get started. The best way to learn is to watch more capable racers and to see how they act at different points around the course.

The most basic and important rule is that the boat on **starboard tack** is always in the right. Being on starboard tack means that your sail is on the left hand side of your boat and you are sitting on the right hand side. If your sail is on the right and you are sitting on the left, then you are on **port tack**, and you have to keep out of the way of anyone sailing on starboard. You will soon gather handy rules such as these, helping you to become competitive on the racing course.

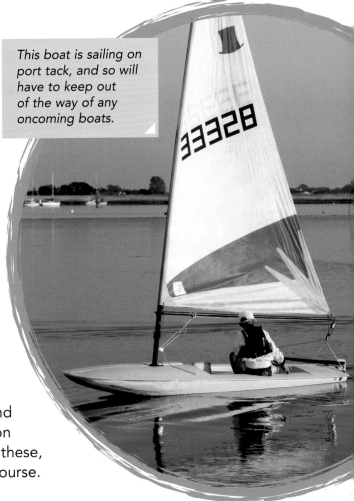

This boat is sailing on port tack, and so will have to keep out of the way of any oncoming boats.

Sailing on starboard tack means you have the right of way over oncoming boats.

Understanding the course

Before you start a race you will have a **briefing** onshore, in which someone will explain where the course is (usually marked out by big floating **buoys** on the water), in what order you need to go around the marks, and on what side of your boat you need to pass by the mark. This is also a chance to ask questions and to get some helpful advice. Everyone is a learner sometime, and other sailors will be happy to help and encourage you.

Sailing challenges!

After you have had your first dinghy sailing experiences, you will want to get involved in all sorts of other challenges, and luckily there are lots out there for you to choose from!

Some larger sailing boats have sleeping quarters and are perfect for family adventures!

Camping on water!

Dinghy sailing is unique as it lets you get to beaches and destinations that you cannot reach by car or bike. This makes it perfect for going on adventures to discover new places and find the perfect picnic spot. Some larger dinghies have room to set up a bed inside, so you can even spend the night onboard. It's a bit like camping – but on the water. Other larger styles of boat are perfect for families, for day trips or longer.

Larger yachts on the open water require bigger teams to handle them.

Yachting challenges

Yachts are just the same as dinghies, except much bigger, and often with an inside section that has beds and a kitchen area. This means that you can stay onboard for much longer periods of time, making them perfect for week-long trips and longer journeys abroad. Up to 20 people are needed to sail some yachts, and everyone on board has an important job to do, making sure the boat sails safely and as quickly as possible. Yacht racing is a very popular, exhilarating sport that is competitive at every level.

Around the world

There is no minimum age requirement for sailing. On 27 August 2009, 17-year-old Mike Perham became the youngest person to sail around the world in a yacht. Although he met up with his dad in a couple of countries along the way, he sailed across the oceans on his own.

Great expeditions

The bigger the boat you sail, the further away from home you can go. While you can sail near the shore in your dinghy, some bigger boats regularly make trips around the globe, spending months at sea and experiencing some of the most extreme conditions on Earth. This may not be something you can tackle straight away, but it would be an amazing dream to have for the future…

Glossary

Beam reach *Sailing at a 90-degree angle to the wind.*

Briefing *The meeting before a sailing race where you are told about the course and when you need to start racing.*

Buoy *A floating ball that marks out the course or an area of water.*

Close-hauled *Sailing as close to the wind as possible.*

Crew *The sailor who controls the jib but does not steer the boat.*

Dagger board *This moves directly up and down, into and out of the water and helps steer the boat and adds balance.*

Dinghy *A small open top boat, often only designed for one sailor at a time.*

Gybing *To change direction with the wind over the back of the boat.*

Helm *The sailor controlling the rudder and mainsail.*

Launch *Removing the boat from its trailer and getting it afloat, ready to sail.*

Mark *The buoys that identify the route you have to race.*

No-go zone *The direction the wind is blowing from. It is not possible to sail in this direction.*

Port tack *This is when you are sailing with the sail on the right hand side of the boat.*

Recover *After a capsize, recovery is the process of correcting the boat so that it is ready to sail again. It can also simply mean to remove the boat from the water.*

Regatta *A big racing event.*

Rigging *The name for the sails and ropes, but it is also the act of setting up the boat before you sail.*

Rudder *This is attached to the tiller and controls the direction of the boat.*

Sheets *In sailing, these are ropes, lines or cables.*

Spinnaker *A extra sail that is used when sailing downwind.*

Starboard tack *This is when you are sailing with the sail on the left hand side of the boat.*

Tacking *To change direction by moving through the wind.*

Toe straps *These are used to hook your feet under when you are sitting on the side of the boat.*

Trailer *A metal frame with wheels used to store and move the boat when on land.*

Training run *Sailing with the wind behind you.*

Trapezing *A harness attached to a wire at the top of the mast, allowing a sailor to get their body weight over the side of the boat.*

Yacht *A large boat, generally with an indoor section and space for a crew of three or more.*

Further information

Books to read

Travelling Wild: Sailing the Great Barrier Reef, Alex Woolf
Wayland (2013)

Skipper's Onboard Knot Guide: Knots, Bends, Hitches and Splices, Adlard Cole
Nautical (2009)

RYA Go Sailing, Claudia Myatt, RYA (2005)

Start Sailing: Beginners Handbook, RYA (2002)

Useful contacts

The Royal Yachting Association (RYA)
www.rya.org.uk

The Welsh Yachting Association (WYA)
www.welshsailing.org

Yachting Australia
www.yachting.org.au

Yachting New Zealand
www.yachtingnz.org.nz

The Royal Yachting Association Northern Ireland
www.ryani.org.uk

The United States Sailing Association
www2.ussailing.org

Websites

www.rya.org.uk

The Royal Yachting Association has a database on their website that lists all the certified training centres in the UK and abroad. You can use their search engine to find the nearest school to you, and learn more about the types of courses they run.

www.dinghysailingmagazine.co.uk

Dinghy Sailing Magazine is a magazine for keen dinghy sailors of all types and abilities.

www.go-sail.co.uk

If you want to find out more about getting into sailing, buying books on the subject or talking to people in the know, this is a great website.

Index

Ainslie, Ben 7

balance 6, 7, 10, 12, 20, 22, 23
beam reach 13, 30
boat 4, 5, 6, 7, 8, 9, 10, 11, 12, 13, 14, 15, 16, 17, 18, 19, 20, 21, 22, 23, 26, 27, 28, 29
  dinghy 5, 7, 24, 26, 28, 29, 30
  double-handed 5, 8, 10, 19, 22
  main parts 10, 11
  single-handed 5, 8, 9, 15, 19
  yacht 5, 29, 30
boom 10, 17, 18, 19
bow 10, 17
buoyancy aid 11, 23

capsize 11, 20, 21, 25
close-hauled 12, 13, 17, 30
clothes 11, 25
club 6, 7, 8, 9, 26, 27
competitions 7, 26–27, 29
crew 5, 19, 23, 30

dagger board 10, 12, 13, 14, 15, 21, 30
direction 4, 5, 11, 12, 13, 14, 16, 17, 18, 19, 23
equipment 9, 10–11, 14, 24

fitness 7

gybing 16, 17, 18, 19, 30

helm 5, 15, 19, 30
hull 10, 15, 21, 23

instructor 8, 9, 26

learning 5, 8, 9, 12, 16, 27

mast 10, 21, 23
muscles 7

no-go zone 12, 30

ocean 4, 6, 29
Olympic Games 7, 26

Perham, Mike 29
port tack 27, 30
professionals 8

racing 4, 5, 7, 24, 26–27, 29
rigging 14, 15, 30
river 4, 5, 6
ropes 10, 11, 14, 15, 17, 18, 19, 21, 23
  mainsheet 10, 14, 15, 18, 19, 21, 23
  painter 10, 15
Royal Yachting Association 9, 24
rudder 4, 11, 12, 14, 21, 30
rules 26, 27

safety 8, 11, 14, 24, 25, 29
sail 4, 5, 7, 10, 12, 13, 14, 15, 16, 17, 18, 19, 20, 21, 22, 23, 27
  jib 10

mainsail 10, 12, 14, 15, 17, 23
  spinnaker 23, 30
sailing school 6, 9, 10, 11, 13, 24
skills 6, 7, 27
speed 4, 5, 13, 16, 22, 26, 29
starboard tack 27, 30
steering 4, 5, 9, 10, 11, 15, 17, 19
stern 11, 17
swimming 8, 11, 20, 21

tacking 16, 17, 18, 19, 30
technique 8, 9, 12–13, 14–15, 16–17, 18–19, 20–21, 22–23
tiller 11, 14, 15, 16, 17. 18, 19, 21
toe straps 15, 20, 30
trailer 5, 30
training 6, 9, 27
training run 13, 30
trapezing 22, 23, 30

warming up 7
water 4, 5, 6, 7, 8, 9, 10, 11, 12, 14, 15, 20, 21, 24, 25, 26, 27, 28
weather 8, 24
wetsuit 11
wind 4, 8, 12, 13, 14, 15, 16, 17, 18, 19, 20, 21, 22, 23, 25